FULL CIRCLE

The 209 Days That United the World and Saved an Olympic Sport

T.R. Foley
Photo Editor: Tony Rotundo

Introduction

"Almost certainly wrestling is the oldest sport of mankind ... It came to town with the Olympiads of Ancient Greece and went back to the country after the decline of Rome — there to remain, at least in greatest part, for nearly two thousand years. Preponderantly in and because of the country the sport has lived on in the general manner of pasture bluets, or field daisies, or other more or less global and substantially invincible wildflowers. Time and time again pasture bluets can be and have been burned away by the heavy hoofs or close-grazing herds. Yet with mystic stubbornness and effectiveness the pasture bluets somehow rise and bloom again. Wrestling is like that. It thrives, meets apparent destruction or widespread abandonment only to rise again, taking resurrection from a good and folkish earth. This has come to pass in many nations and it keeps happening in our own."

—Charles Morrow Wilson, *The Magnificent Scufflers*, 1959

Wrestling has been part of every summer Olympics since 1904. It is a simple and status-free sport, open to the rich and the poor, male and female. Egalitarian in its acceptance and fair in its rules, "Man's Oldest Sport" has appeared for centuries in cultures around the world. From the Ancient Greek Games to the mud pits of modern India, wrestling has proven to be an inextricable part of the human experience.

Despite wrestling's deep and longstanding connection to the Olympic movement, the Executive Board of the International Olympic Committee met in Lausanne, Switzerland, on February 12, 2013, and voted wrestling out of the Olympic Games. The Executive Board was charged with reducing the number of core Olympic sports to 25, which meant one needed to be trimmed. Wrestling was their choice.

The IOC stressed components of modern Olympic membership in which wrestling has been vulnerable for decades. The sport of wrestling wasn't judged on its long history or modern day importance within developing nations, but on metrics of television viewership, gender equity, and institutional functionality. All were subpar and trending downward.

Although it came as a shock to the worldwide wrestling community, the IOC had announced the vote several months earlier. The 15-member Executive Board had even welcomed weeks of heavy politicking by other at-risk Olympic sports, most notably tae kwon do and modern pentathlon. Faced with an existential threat, those sports sent brigades of fast-talking, influential lobbyists to Lausanne to argue for their survival.

Wrestling, under the direction of international governing body FILA and president Raphael Martinetti, chose not to lobby members of the IOC.

According to the vote, wrestling's Olympic banishment would begin after the 2016 Games in Rio de Janeiro, Brazil. The full session of the IOC would first have to ratify the recommendations, but pundits within the international sports scene believed wrestling stood little chance of Olympic reinstatement. The logic was simple: The IOC would never restore a sport it eliminated a few months earlier.

Despite the finality of their original decision, the IOC Executive Board left open a loophole by which the sport of wrestling could regain its Olympic status—allowing wrestling to apply for status as a "provisional sport" at the 2020 and 2024 Olympic Games. Although typically reserved for sports seeking first-time inclusion in the Olympic program, the provisional route meant that wrestling would have to compete against seven other sports over two rounds of voting. The first vote was May 28 and would trim the list from eight sports to three. The final vote would occur September 8 in Buenos Aires, Argentina, and decide which sport would be added to the Olympics. Wrestling had 209 days to fight for its Olympic life.

For many in the wrestling community, the IOC Executive Board's decision represented the elimination of the sport's crowning achievement. Unlike football, soccer, and basketball, which have professional leagues with worldwide championships, wrestling is largely focused on Olympic gold. There is no lateral championship or league title outside of the annual FILA-run World Championships. Without the Olympics, national governing bodies in poor countries would pull funding for their wrestling programs and eliminate opportunities for their wrestlers to compete in any championship, home or abroad.

FILA scrambled to answer for their failures and develop mechanisms for exerting influence on the IOC. As the ramifications of the decision became clear, frustration with the organization's leadership mounted. Although they were tasked with keeping up good relations with the IOC, it was evident FILA had been inactive in the lead-up to the vote, leaving the sport vulnerable to an Olympic collapse. Suffering from organizational ineptitude and facing a stalwart IOC, the world had little reason to expect an Olympic comeback.

But the wrestling community turned their anger into action, and, within hours, phones calls, emails, and texts between wrestlers began. The largest mobilization effort in the sport's history was underway. From Moscow to Dakar, Ulaanbaatar to New York, business leaders, politicians, and Olympic athletes began to pool their resources. By the time the sun rose on February 13, the wrestling community was on course to create the largest sport-reinstatement campaign in Olympic history.

There were only 208 days left to Save Olympic Wrestling.

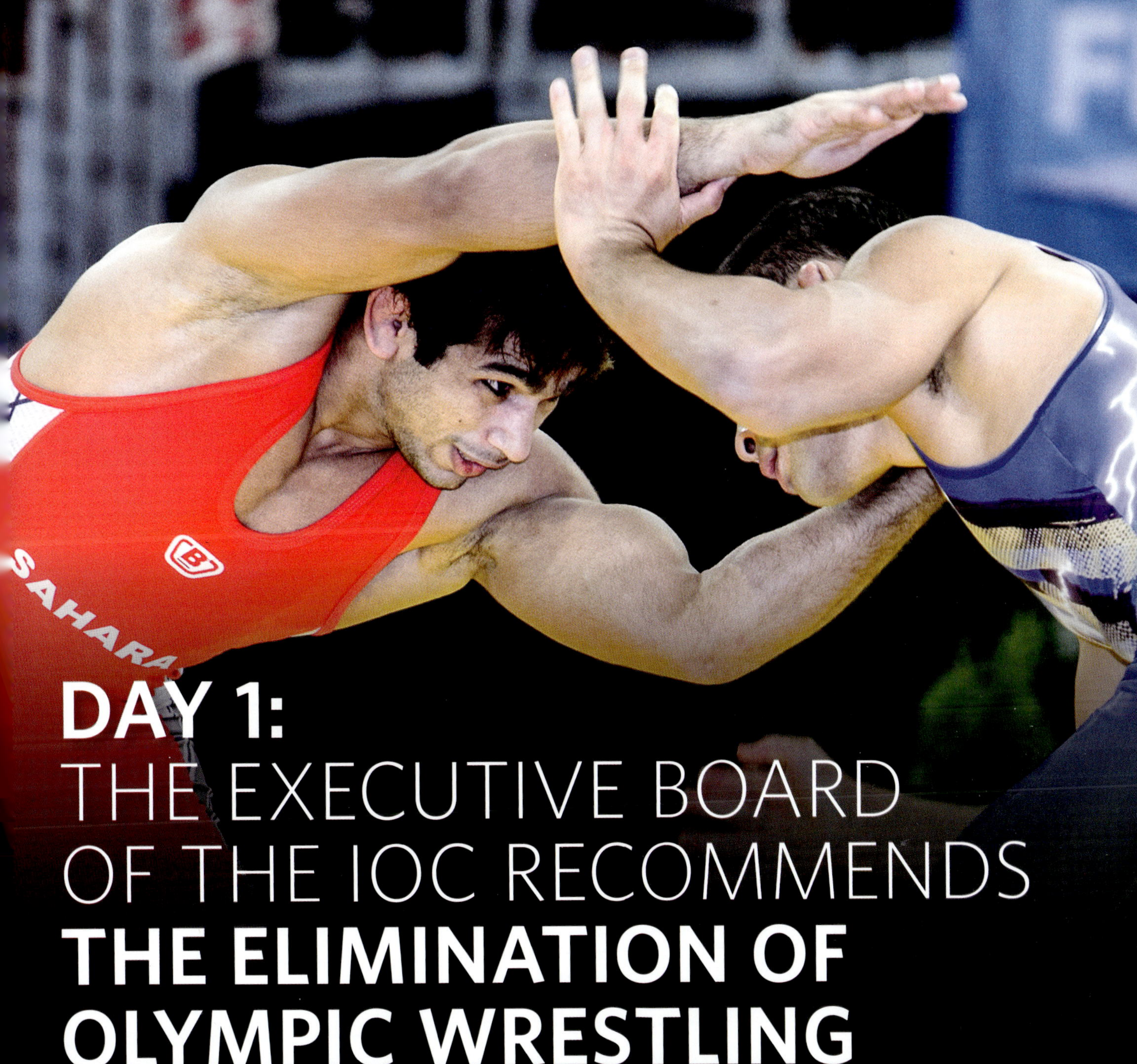

DAY 1:
THE EXECUTIVE BOARD OF THE IOC RECOMMENDS
THE ELIMINATION OF OLYMPIC WRESTLING

February 12, Lausanne, Switzerland

In a decision that shocks the worldwide wrestling community, the Executive Board of the International Olympic Committee (IOC) recommends that wrestling be dropped as a core sport of the Olympic program following the 2016 Games. The recommendations will be put up for vote on September 8 in front of the 125th Session of the IOC in Buenos Aires, Argentina.

DAY 3:
U.S. CONGRESSMEN
INTRODUCE HOUSE RESOLUTION 71.

February 14, Washington D.C.

U.S. Congressmen Dave Loebsack (R-IA), Jim Jordan (R-OH), Tim Walz (D-MN), Bruce Braley (D-IA), Steve King (R-IA) and Tom Latham (R-IA) introduce House Resolution 71 opposing the IOC executive board's recommendation. Politicians from both sides of the aisle release statements in support of Olympic wrestling and help pass state legislation to make their opposition part of the public record.

BILL & JIM SCHERR ESTABLISH THE **COMMITTEE FOR THE PRESERVATION OF OLYMPIC WRESTLING**

February 14, Chicago, Illinois

Bill Scherr, president of World Sport Chicago, and his brother Jim, former CEO of the United States Olympic Committee, form an ad-hoc committee of USA Wrestling known as the Committee for the Preservation of Olympic Wrestling (CPOW). The committee becomes the central location for recruiting financial resources and talent for the fight to keep wrestling in the Olympics.

(Left) Jim Scherr, former CEO of the United States Olympic Committee.

DAY 8:
CPOW RECRUITS TALENT, **ORGANIZES COMMITTEE STRUCTURE**

February 19, New York, New York

CPOW completes its working structure of committees and subcommittees bringing together former Olympic athletes, politicians and celebrities. The committee will raise more than $2 million and become the centerpiece of the American effort to keep wrestling in the Olympic games.

Pictured: (Top) Actor Tom Arnold, former UFC Champion Randy Couture and actor Billy Baldwin. (Bottom) Noel Thompson, USA Wrestling president James Ravannack and actor Billy Baldwin.

DAY 9:
VALENTIN JORDANOV
RETURNS OLYMPIC GOLD

February 20, Sofia, Bulgaria

Bulgarian Wrestling Federation president Valentin Jordanov returns his 1996 Olympic gold medal in protest of the IOC's decision to remove wrestling from the Olympics. Though FILA would later ask that their athletes find other avenues of protest, Jordanov's powerful gesture makes headlines around the world.

DAY 11:
MEN'S FREESTYLE AND GRECO-ROMAN **WORLD CUP**

February 22, Tehran, Iran

Though at political odds, the fight to Save Olympic Wrestling serves as a common interest among leaders from Russia, Iran and the United States. The three nations join five others in Tehran to compete in the 2013 World Cup in men's freestyle and Greco-Roman. At the end of the competition, Iranian president Mahmoud Ahmadinejad stands with members of the American freestyle team for a photo that will be seen around the world.

"OLYMPICS WITHOUT WRESTLING? NEVER, NEVER..."

READE THE BANNERS SURROUNDING THE PRESIDENT OF IRAN.

Olympic Champion Jordan Burroughs (USA) shakes hands with Iranian fans after his World Cup victory.

LALOVIC MEETS WITH
IOC VICE PRESIDENT THOMAS BACH

March 1, Frankfurt, Germany

Acting FILA President Nenad Lalovic meets with IOC Vice President and German Olympic Committee President Thomas Bach in Frankfurt, Germany. Bach advises FILA about potential measures to develop wrestling and about the presentation of FILA to the IOC Executive Board in May. He also stresses the fairness of competition rules, the participation of athletes in the FILA decision-making process and the necessity of a global development program for wrestling. Lalovic and Bach also discuss the promotion of women's wrestling and the future involvement of women in FILA governance.

Bach also congratulates Lalovic and FILA. "The plans to develop wrestling better, to make it more attractive for youth world-wide and globally more popular, together with the application of the IOC principles of good governance are the right approach."

DAY 22:
ASSOCIATION OF NATIONAL OLYMPIC COMMITTEES
PRESIDENT OFFERS SUPPORT

March 5, Kuwait City, Kuwait

Kuwait's Sheikh Ahmad Al-Fahad Al-Sabah, leader of the Association of National Olympic Committees, writes a letter in support of FILA and the preservation of Olympic wrestling. Though not as well-known as IOC president Jacques Rogge, the Sheikh is one of the most influential voices in international sports.

DAY 24:
LALOVIC MEETS WITH IOC PRESIDENT ROGGE

March 7, Lausanne, Switzerland

Acting FILA President Nenad Lalovic meets with IOC President Jacques Rogge to discuss the Olympic future of wrestling. "The meeting was very cordial and helpful," says Lalovic. "Our objective was to listen and learn from the discussion with President Rogge and I am very pleased with the result."

"Every sport, including wrestling, has to earn its place on the Olympic program. We know this will take hard work and are ready for it. Our goal is to make a great sport better and to be stronger partners in the Olympic family."

DAY 25:
KETCHUM BUILDS PR CAMPAIGN

March 8, New York, New York

Roger Frizzell, chairman of the PR committee formed by CPOW, finalizes an agreement with Ketchum to create a robust PR initiative aiming to increase public awareness of the Save Olympic Wrestling campaign. The organization also coordinates the hiring of communications specialist Joe Favorito as a senior consultant for strategic communications and digital marketing.

Pictured: (Left) Ehsan Lashgari (IRI) and Taimuraz Friev Naskidaeva (ESP) tie up at 84 kg. (Right) 2012 **Olympic Champion Jordan Burroughs.**

DAY 26:
BOB CONDRON JOINS FILA AS DIRECTOR OF MEDIA OPERATIONS

March 9, Corsier-Sur-Vevey, Switzerland

Legendary media operative Bob Condron moves to Switzerland to improve FILA's media operations and promote President Lalovic's interactions with the press. Condron, who worked in the media department at the United States Olympic Committee for more than 30 years, has worked 15 Olympic games and maintains vital relationships with reporters from the Associated Press, Reuters, and many others.

DAY 36:
CPOW LAUNCHES 2020 VISION

March 19, New York, New York

CPOW and USA Wrestling launch "2020 Vision," which highlights the international effort to raise money and awareness for the battle to Keep Olympic Wrestling. King of the Mountain Sports (KOM), a marketing firm in Colorado Springs selected by CPOW and USA Wrestling for marketing assistance, takes a leadership role in the 2020 Vision movement. KOM also manages the KeepOlympicWrestling.com site and helps it become the nerve central for wrestling fans looking donate to the cause or read updates on the progress towards reinstatement.

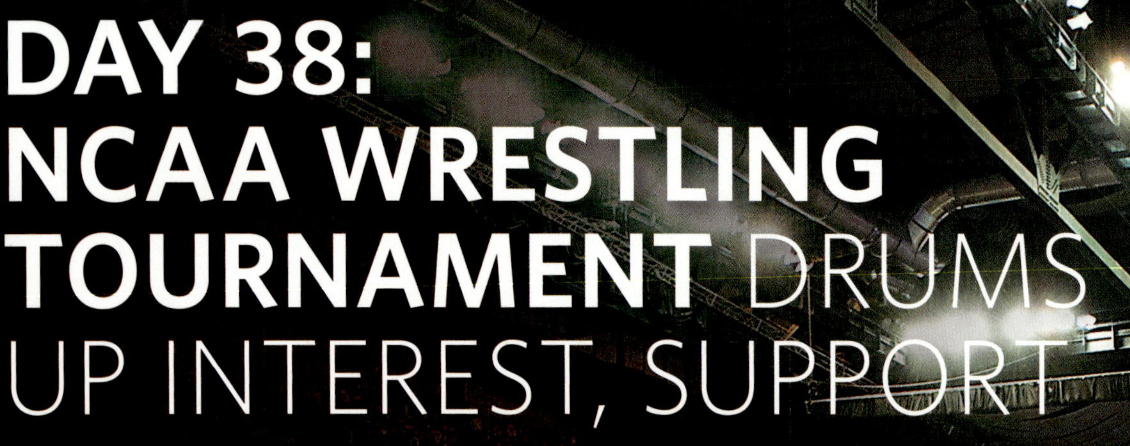

DAY 38:
NCAA WRESTLING TOURNAMENT DRUMS
UP INTEREST, SUPPORT

March 21, Des Moines, Iowa

One of the most visible wrestling events in the world, the NCAA Division I Wrestling tournament becomes an important meeting place for leaders of CPOW and fans interested in providing support.

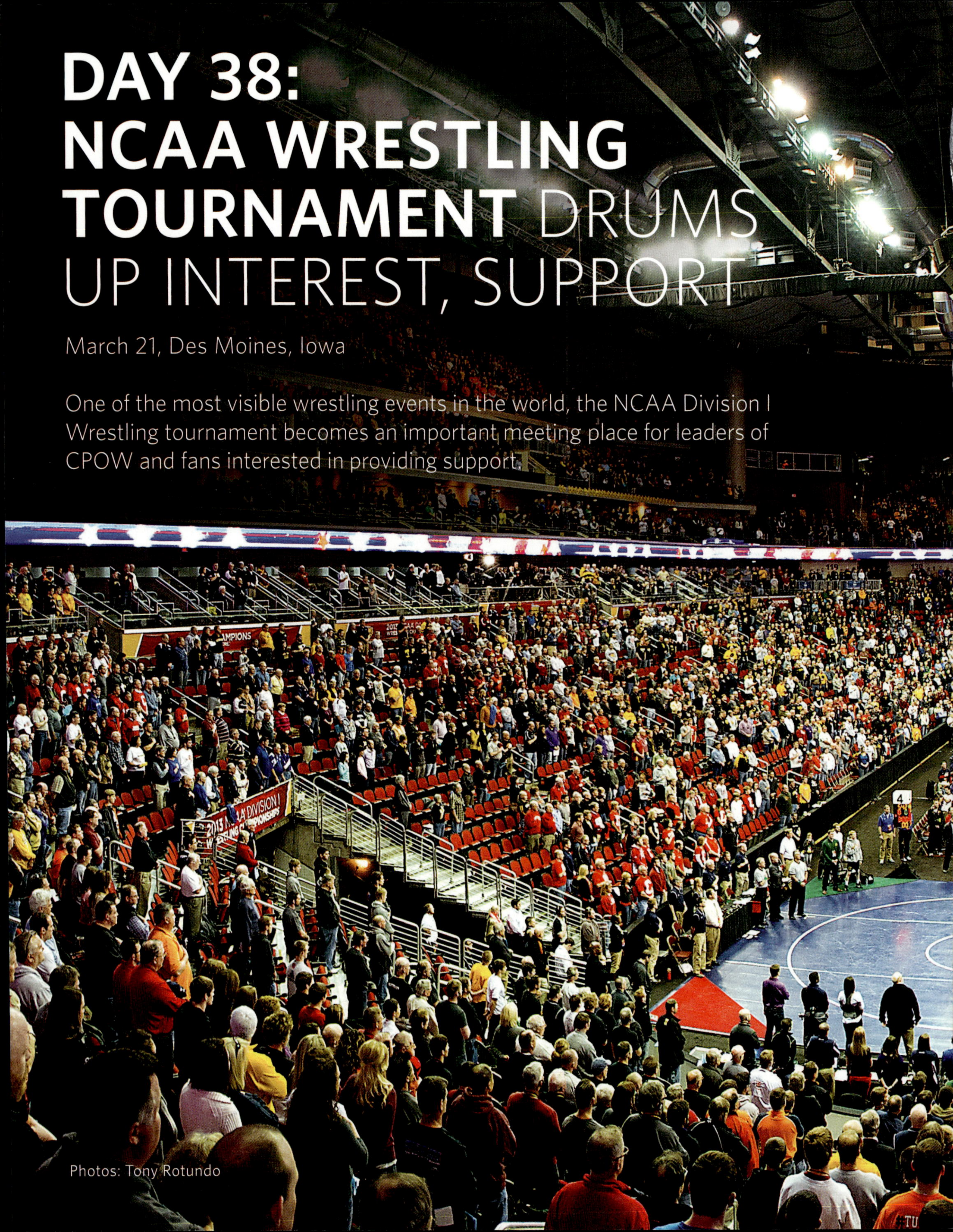

Photos: Tony Rotundo

2013 NCAA champion Kendric Maple (Oklahoma) looks for points against K. Undrakhbayar (Citadel) at 141 lbs.

Four-time NCAA champion Kyle Dake (Cornell) looks for a takedown against David Taylor (Penn State) in the 165 lb. finals.

PENN
STATE

Nico Megaloudis (Penn State) defends an attack by Jesse Delgado (Illinois) in the finals of the 125 lb. weight class.

DAY 38:
ARMEN NAZARYAN
ENDS HUNGER STRIKE

March 21, Tbilisi, Georgia

Two-time Olympic gold medalist Armen Nazaryan ends the hunger strike he began on March 2 to protest the IOC's Feb. 12 recommendations to eliminate wrestling from the Olympic Games.

DAY 39:
CPOW PRESS CONFERENCE
CREATES BUZZ

March 22, Des Moines, Iowa

CPOW Chairman Bill Scherr, U.S. Congressman Jim Jordan and Olympic champions Dan Gable and Jordan Burroughs host a press conference to answer questions about CPOW's efforts and the process for Olympic reinstatement.

Pictured: (Middle) USA Wrestling Communications Director Gary Abbott, CPOW Chairman Bill Scherr, Congressman Jim Jordan, and legendary wrestler Dan Gable address the media at the NCAA Division I tournament. (Bottom) 2012 Olympic Champion Jake Varner, USA National team head wrestling coach Zeke Jones, James Ravannack and 2012 Olympic Champion Jordan Burroughs.

DAY 42:
EUROPEAN CHAMPIONSHIPS
HIGHLIGHT INTERNATIONAL SUPPORT.

March 25, Tbilisi, Georgia

The European Championships are the second major international tournament since the announcement of the IOC's decision. Fans, wrestlers and coaches from across Europe join together to support the fight with tee-shirts, banners, press conferences and quotes through media.

Pictured: (Left) Suemeyya Sezer (TUR) finishes a takedown against Jacqueline Schellin (GER) in the bronze medal match at 48 kg. (Below) Freestyle wrestler Aniuar Geduev (RUS) looks for a high amplitude throw against Grigor Grigoryan (ARM) in the 74 kg semi-finals.

Photos: Martin Gabor/FILA

Vladislav Baitsaev (RUS) looks for the takedown against Elizbar Odikadze of (GEO) during 96 kg freestyle action at the 2013 European Championships.

Pictured: Markus Kecht

Pictured: Andrew Craig

DAY 43:
CPOW AND FILA HIRE **INFLUENTIAL CONSULTANTS**

March 26 ,Corsier-Sur-Vevey, Switzerland

CPOW and FILA hire leading sport and media consultants from Teneo and TSE to offer consulting support throughout the lobbying process. TSE will develop a strategic plan for the sport of wrestling worldwide with markers at one, three and five years. Well-known strategist Andrew Craig is hired as a Senior Advisor for International Relations, along with Markus Kecht and Stratos Safioleas who help ensure vital communication with members of the IOC and the wrestling community.

NIGERIA SUPPORTS THE KEEP OLYMPIC WRESTLING MOVEMENT

March 28, Abuja, Nigeria

Under the direction and support of Olympic gold medalist Daniel Igali, the Federal Government of Nigeria comes out in favor of keeping wrestling as an Olympic Sport. Though a developing nation for international wrestling, Nigeria's second-most popular sport is traditional wrestling.

DAY 46:
LALOVIC MEETS WITH THE **EUROPEAN OLYMPIC COMMITTEE**

March 29, Rome, Italy

In an effort to broaden FILA's influence among the powerful Olympic committees in Europe, acting FILA president Nenad Lalovic travels to Rome to meet with members of the European Olympic Committee.

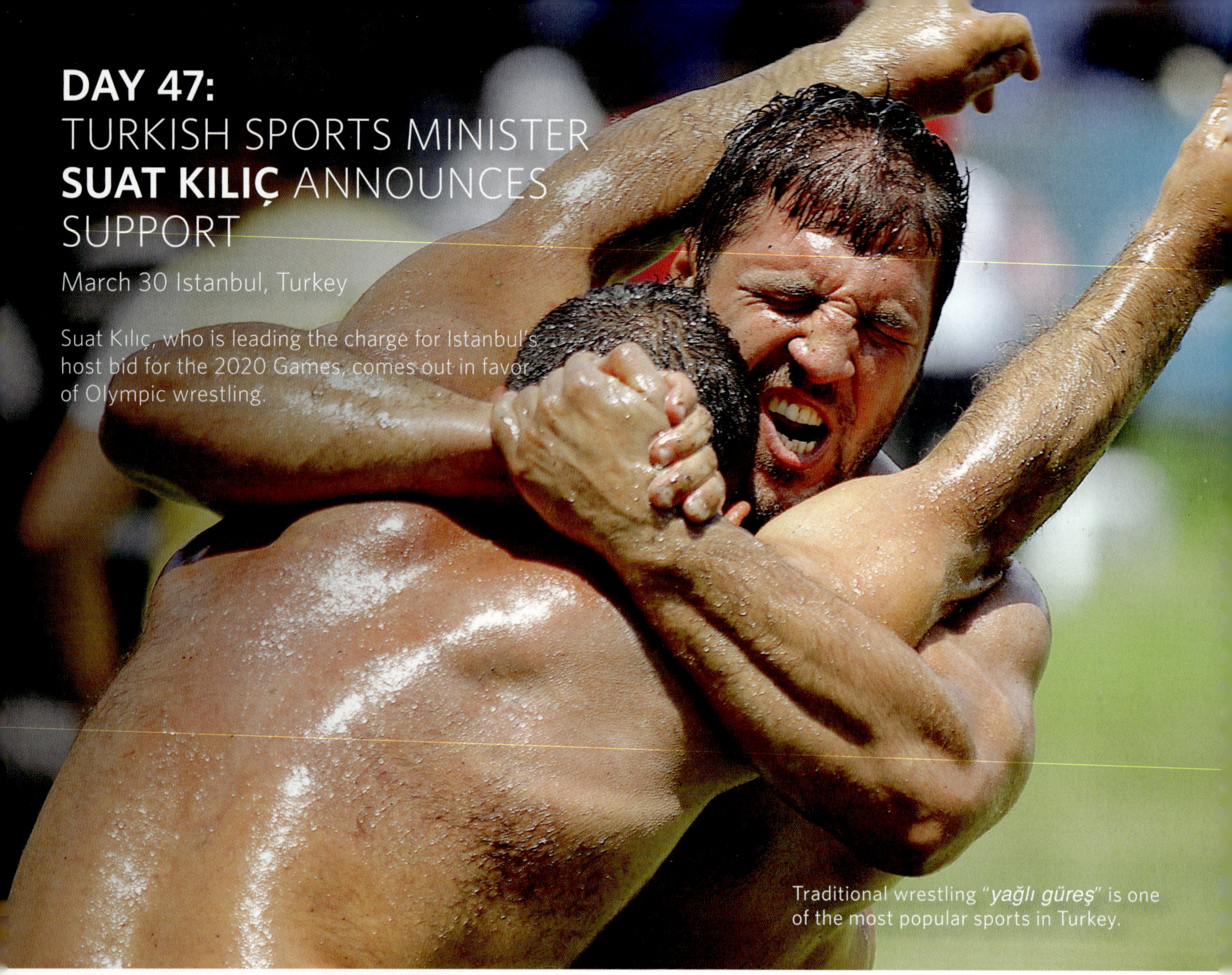

DAY 47: TURKISH SPORTS MINISTER SUAT KILIÇ ANNOUNCES SUPPORT

March 30 Istanbul, Turkey

Suat Kılıç, who is leading the charge for Istanbul's host bid for the 2020 Games, comes out in favor of Olympic wrestling.

Traditional wrestling "*yağlı güreş*" is one of the most popular sports in Turkey.

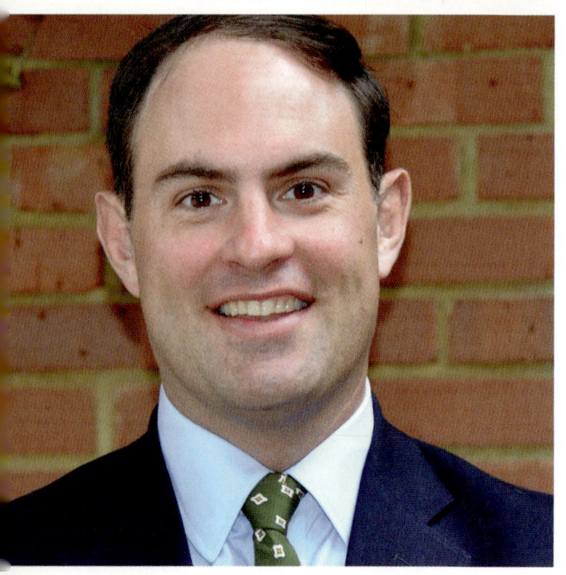

DAY 49: WES BATTLE NAMED CPOW CHIEF OF STAFF

April 1, Washington D.C.

Retired Naval aviator Wes Battle is hired to help manage CPOW's growing staff and budget needs. The former University of Virginia wrestler helps organize millions of dollars in new donations and plans several international events.

BENDER RECRUITS
SAVE OLYMPIC WRESTLING COALITION

April 2, Colorado Springs, Colorado

Citing a need for improved international cooperation and communication, USA Wrestling president Rich Bender forms an international coalition of more than 50 National Wrestling Federations. Members of the coalition agree to support the FILA lobbying effort within the IOC, mobilize energy and resources in their country in support of keeping wrestling on the Olympic program, and promote Olympic wrestling through the upcoming World Wrestling Month.

DAY 51:
LALOVIC MEETS WITH
BULGARIAN PRESIDENT
ROSEN PLEVNIEV

April 3, Sofia, Bulgaria

Acting FILA president Nenad Lalovic
meets with Bulgarian president Rosen
Plevniev in Sofia to recruit his help in the
ongoing campaign to keep wrestling in
the Olympics. Plevniev, whose country
ranks as one of the world's most consistent
Olympic performers in wrestling, offers
his assistance and joins several other
heads of state in making statements
and direct appeals to the IOC on behalf
of FILA and the sport of wrestling.

You are posting, commenting, and liking as Keep Wrestling in the Olympics — Change to Harris Kalofonos
Admin Panel
Notifications 3   Edit Page   Build Audience
2020 Vision
Wrestling
Keep
the Dream
Alive
2020 Vision
Wrestling
Keep
the Dream
Alive
Keep Wrestling in the Olympics
Community Page about USA Wrestling

DAY 51:
CPOW
CALL TO
ACTION

April 3, New York, New York

CPOW leaders make a
direct appeal to the wrestling
community to increase the
visibility and volume of their
support.

DAY 52:
MIKE NOVOGRATZ
PENS LETTER TO THE WRESTLING COMMUNITY

April 4, New York, New York

CPOW spokesperson Mike Novogratz writes a letter to the wrestling community asking for increased support during Phase I of the campaign.

"We are gaining momentum, but we cannot do it alone," writes Novogratz. "We need the continued support, fund raising and help from the wrestling community now more than ever... We have already shown the passion and commitment that is inherent in wrestlers to fight for what is right, but we also need to motivate others to join us. In other words, we have done well in the first period, but we have to finish out the match strong."

Novogratz, the principal and director of Fortress Investment Group, and a former captain of the Princeton wrestling team, is one of the campaign's most influential fundraisers recruiting assistance from Wall Street while also making significant personal contributions to the movement.

DAY 53:
GREECE WRESTLING FEDERATION
JOINS FIGHT

April 5, Athens, Greece

Noting the country's history as the birthplace of the Ancient Olympics, the Greece Wrestling Federation pledges its support to the Save Olympic Wrestling movement. In addition to the Ancient Olympic games, Greece also hosted the first modern Olympics held 1896 in Athens.

KERIMOV

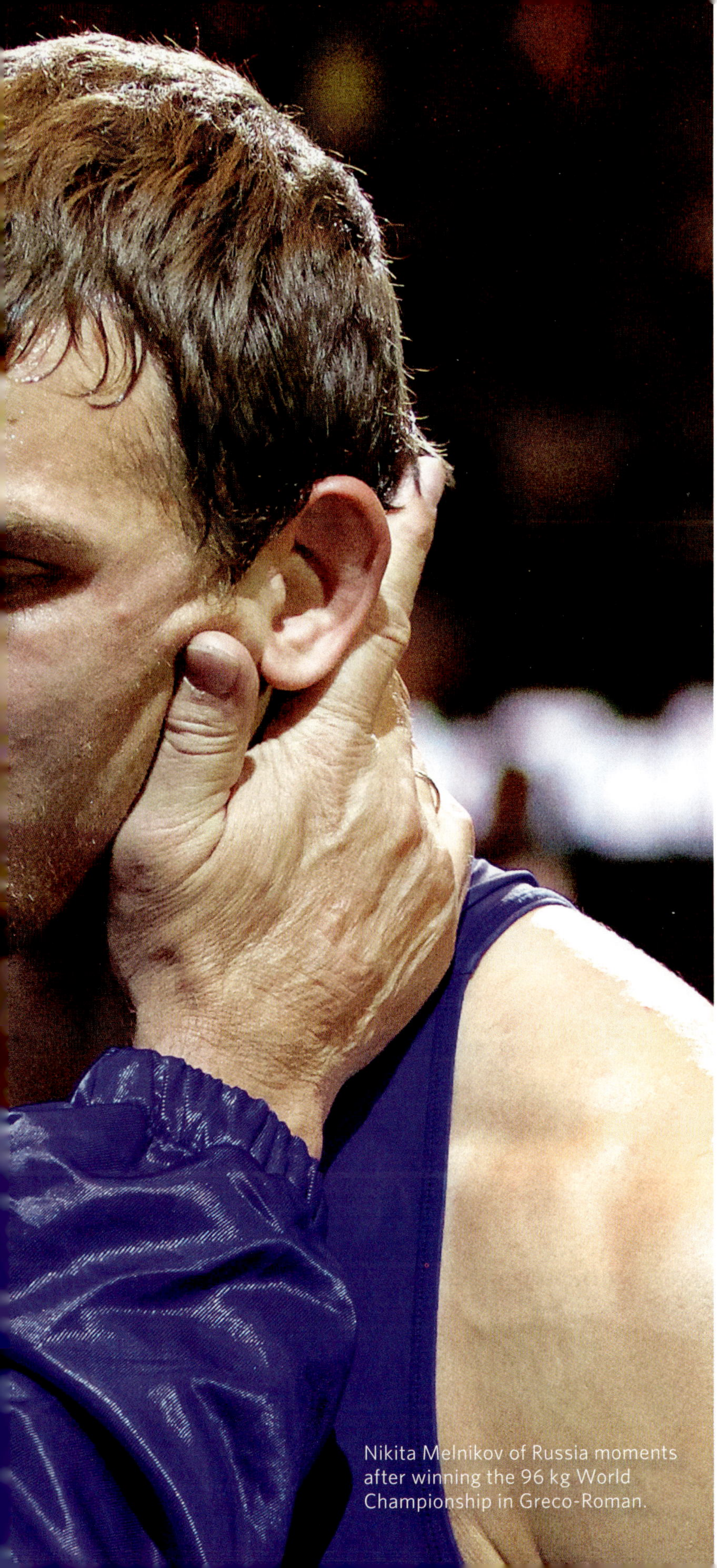

Nikita Melnikov of Russia moments after winning the 96 kg World Championship in Greco-Roman.

DAY 54: RUSSIA BECOMES CENTER OF ACTIVITY, AWARENESS

April 6, Russia

The Russian leg of the global campaign for World Wrestling Month, entitled "Wrestling! To be continued ... " is launched in four cities: Moscow, Kaliningrad, Cheboksary and Kyzyl.

Legendary athletes, Russian politicians and cultural figures back the sport's effort to stay on Olympic program. Wrestling Federation of Russia president Mikhail Mamiashvili and George Brusov, head of FILA's anti-crisis working group, work tirelessly in support of the campaign and are critical at rallying support around Europe and Asia.

Moscow has long been the capital of Olympic wrestling success with the former Soviet Union winning 116 medals, and Russia 51.

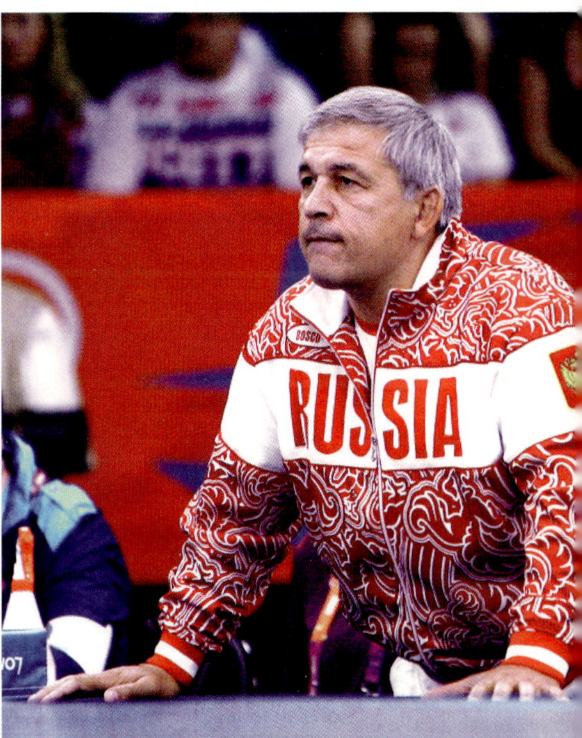

Pictured: (Above) FILA Bureau members Daulet Turlykhanov (KAZ) and Mikhail Mamiashvili (RUS). (Below) Turlykhanov with Mnazakan Iskandaryan (RUS) and Dan Gable (USA) at their 2012 FILA Hall of Fame induction.

General Secretary of the Russian Wrestling Federation George Brusov and three-time Olympic gold medalist Alexander Karelin (RUS)

RUS

DAY 59:
CPOW MEETS
WITH **THE UFC**

April 11, Las Vegas, Nevada

Leaders from CPOW meet in Las Vegas with UFC president Dana White to discuss strategies for increasing attention for the Olympic fight. White pledges his support and follows through by offering several statements on live television and allowing fighters to wear "Save Olympic Wrestling" gear in the Octagon.

Two-time Olympian and UFC light heavyweight Daniel Cormier

DAY 60:
JAPANESE MANAGE **WRITTEN AND ONLINE CAMPAIGNS**

April 12, Tokyo, Japan

The Japanese Wrestling Federation collects more than 920,000 signatures in support of Olympic wrestling. Japan, the birthplace of sumo, is also home to three-time Olympic champions Saori Yoshida and Kaori Icho — the greatest female wrestlers in Olympic history.

The Japanese Wrestling Federation also proves effective at creating social media buzz and generating visually stunning odes to the sport. Photos of the Japanese effort become some of the most-viewed images of the movement.

Support Olympic W
人類最古のスポーツであるレスリングをオリンビ
Support
Olympic
Wreslin
レスリングの五輪競技存続のため
署名にご協力お願いします
サイトからも署名できます ⇨ https://www.change.org/save_wrestling
レスリングの五輪競技
署名にご協力
サイトからも署名で
https://www.change.or
万電氣合

Pictured: (Above) Three-time Olympic champion Saori Yoshida (JPN) and Japanese Wrestling Federation President Tomiaki Fukuda.

DAY 65:
LALOVIC MEETS WITH RUSSIAN PRESIDENT **VLADIMIR PUTIN**

April 17, Sochi, Russia

Acting FILA President Nenad Lalovic and Russian president Vladimir Putin meet at the AIPS Congress in Sochi to discuss strategies for reinstating wrestling as an Olympic sport. In their meetings Putin reaffirms his commitment to the sport and pledges increased involvement as the IOC executive board meetings in St. Petersburg draw closer.

DAY 66:
2013 ASIAN CHAMPIONSHIPS

April 18, New Delhi, India

The 2013 Asian Championships become another showcase of international cooperation during the Save Olympic Wrestling movement. India, one of the fastest-improving programs in the world, takes the team title in men's freestyle as wrestlers from around the region use the tournament to voice their support for the sport.

DAY 69:
US OPEN AND CPOW
PRESS CONFERENCE

April 21, Las Vegas, Nevada

Wrestling leaders from around the United States descend on Las Vegas to help generate awareness for the event and the upcoming vote in St. Petersburg.

Pictured: (Right) Legendary American wrestler and coach Dan Gable. (Below) Traditional Mongolian wrestlers compete at Naadam, the country's annual wrestling tournament held every July in cities across the country.

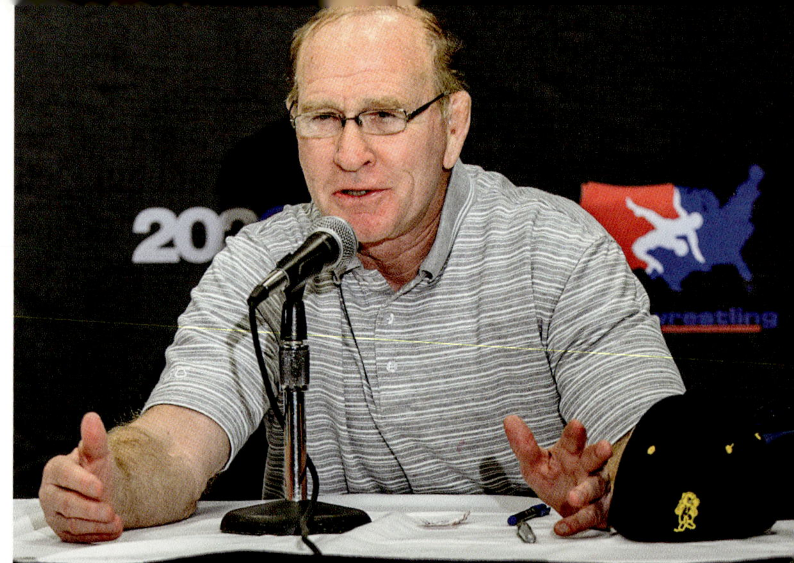

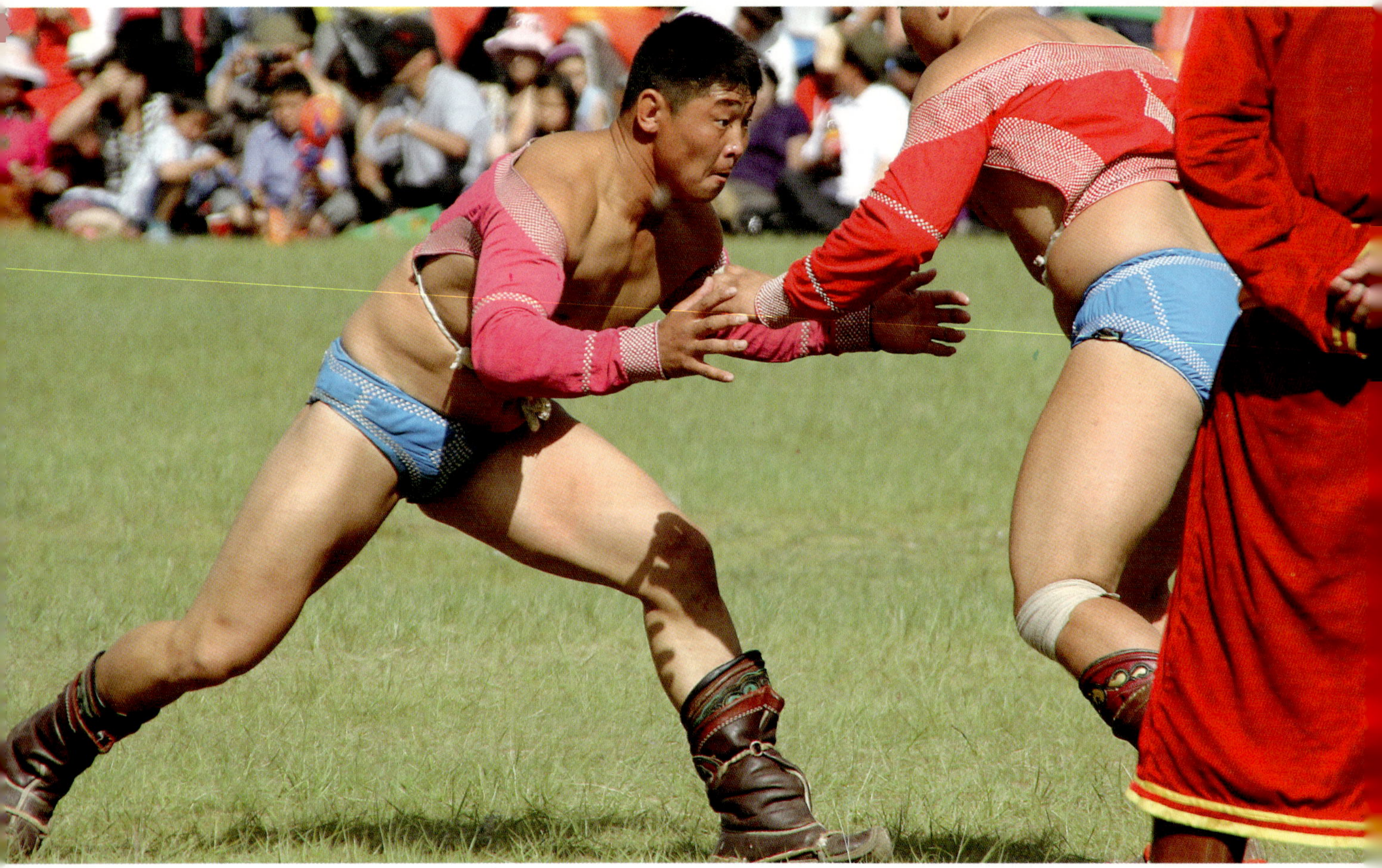

DAY 72:
15TH ANNUAL IOC "SPORT FOR ALL WORLD" CONFERENCE

April 24, Lima, Peru

FILA Bureau members Stan Dziedzic and Jim Scherr head to Lima to talk with IOC members and drum up support for wrestling's Olympic fight. Though often dismissed as a combat sport, Dziedzic and Scherr help explain the role wrestling plays in conflict resolution and creating equal opportunities for women and ethnic minorities in developing countries.

DAY 79: WORLD WRESTLING MONTH

May 1, Worldwide

One of the most important initiatives of the entire movement, CPOW and FILA help coordinate "World Wrestling Month," 31 days of tournaments and events meant to drive interest in the sport in the weeks and days leading up to May 18 vote in St. Petersburg.

Russia launches, "Wrestling! To be continued," and creates major wrestling activities in the cities of Moscow, Kalingrad, Cheboksary and Kyzyl. Their efforts also include the National Youth Greco-Roman Championships in Moscow, featuring teams from 69 regions of the country.

The Americans and Canadians also create several specialized events in the hopes of creating inter-national news.

Pictured: (Above) USA Wrestling Executive Director Rich Bender. (Left) USA Wrestling President James Ravannack.

A traditional wrestler from Senegal (L) looks to defend the takedown attempt of his opponent from Niger.

DAY 80: AFRICAN CHAMPIONSHIPS

May 2, N'Djamena, Chad

Acting FILA President Nenad Lalovic meets with leaders of several national governing bodies from around Africa and offers support for increased development of the sport on the continent. Lalovic also gives remarks that mention his hope for Africa's continued improvement at the international level.

The African Championships are also the showcase for FILA's first-ever African Traditional Wrestling Championships, which allows for traditional wrestlers from around Africa to compete in a version of takedown-only African-themed wrestling. More than 20,000 spectators watch the finals match between Chad and Senegal.

Pictured: (Below) Director of FILA Development for Africa, Didier Favori.

Chad won its first-ever match in Greco-Roman wrestling at the 2013 African Championships, bringing hope for that country's Olympic wrestling future.

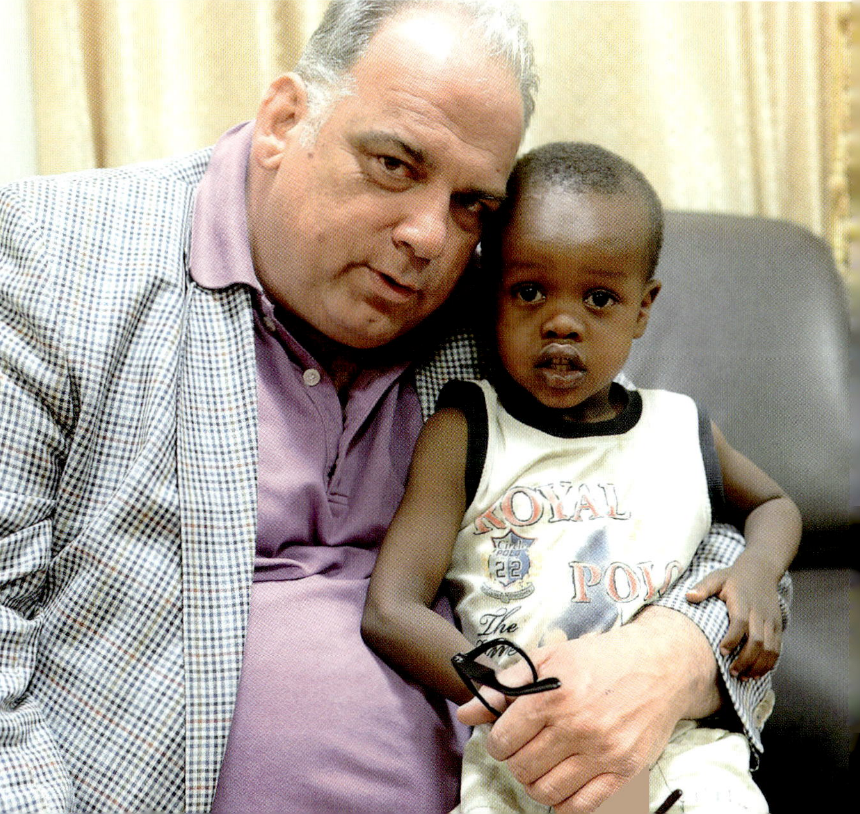

Pictured: University of Maryland
head wrestling coach Kerry McCoy.

DAY 87:
PRESENTATION TO US AID

May 9, Washington D.C.

Bill Scherr and Olympic champions Rulon Gardner and Henry Cejudo join University of Maryland head wrestling coach Kerry McCoy and Olympic bronze medalist Clarissa Chun to present the benefits of wrestling to the US AID at the Capital Rotunda in Washington DC. The event brings together foreign aid workers and leaders of the wrestling community for brainstorming on how to increase wrestling's role in developing countries.

Gardner, Chun, Scherr, Cejudo
and McCoy in the Capitol Rotunda.

Olympic gold medalist Henry Cejudo competing
in the 2012 US Olympic Team trials.

Regional tournaments like the Mongolian Open show support for the movement and wrestling's resiliency during a time of uncertainty. The sport of wrestling is competed in 177 countries and tournaments like the Mongolian Open continued to showcase wrestling talent even as the sport's Olympic future is in jeopardy.

Mongolian fans are treated to high amplitude, intense wrestling.

Photos: C. Ganbat

Medal stand for 59 kg in
women's freestyle.

B. Ankhbayar (MGL)
celebrates his gold medal
performance at 74 kg.

DAY 92:
UN LUNCHEON

May 14, New York, New York

Wrestling leaders from CPOW and FILA meet at the United Nations in Manhattan to discuss the importance of Olympic wrestling around the world. Acting FILA President Nenad Lalovic attends a press conference where each team's athletes for the following day's competition weigh-in and are introduced to the media. Lalovic tells reporters, "We are dedicated to reforming our sport and making FILA a more pro-active and responsible organization. We will do everything we can to address the IOC's concerns and ensure that wrestling remains a part of the Olympic Games."

DAY 93:
RUMBLE ON THE RAILS

May 15, New York, New York

In an effort to create a marquee event in the media capital of the world, CPOW and FILA partner with Beat the Streets to host teams from Russia, Iran and the United States at Grand Central Terminal's Vanderbilt Hall in New York City. Billed "The Rumble On The Rails" the event sells out of tickets and airs live on the NBC Sports Network.

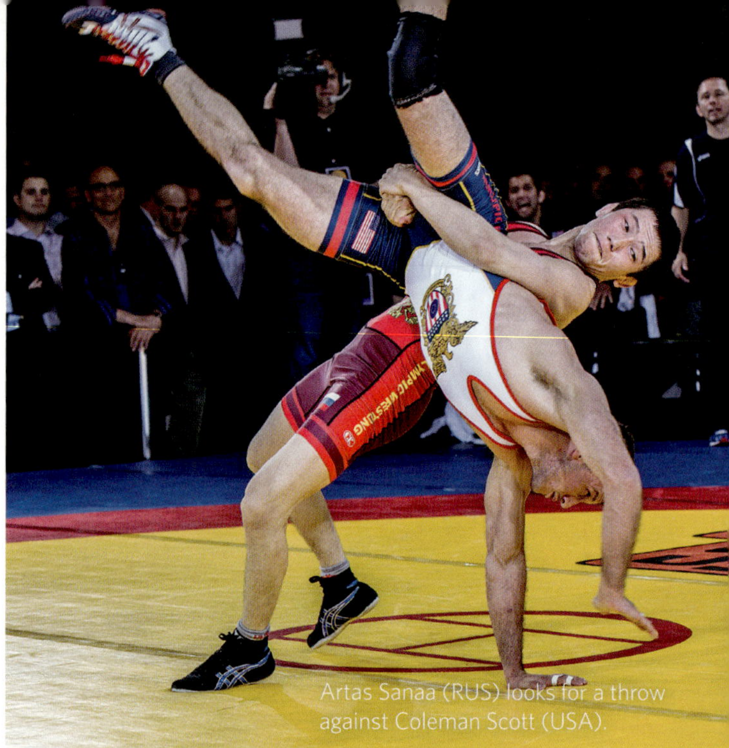

Artas Sanaa (RUS) looks for a throw against Coleman Scott (USA).

Logan Stieber (USA) lifts Opan Sat (RUS).

Mehdi Taghavi (IRI) on a single leg against Kellen Russell (USA).

Kyle Dake (USA) goes big during a takedown attempt against Hassan Tahmasebi (IRI).

Photos: John Sachs

Helen Maroulis (USA) battles Irina Kisel (RUS). Maroulis would go on to earn a second period fall.

DAY 96:
FILA EXTRAORDINARY CONGRESS VOTES NEW RULES, PRESIDENT

May 18, Moscow, Russia

At a special Extraordinary Congress in Moscow FILA begins the process of voting on significant changes to the rules and governance of international wrestling. All 177 national federations are invited to the Russian capital to vote on the changes. Acting President Nenad Lalovic is elected as the seventh president of FILA and the proposed rule changes are approved by the FILA as athletes and women were given greater roles within the organization

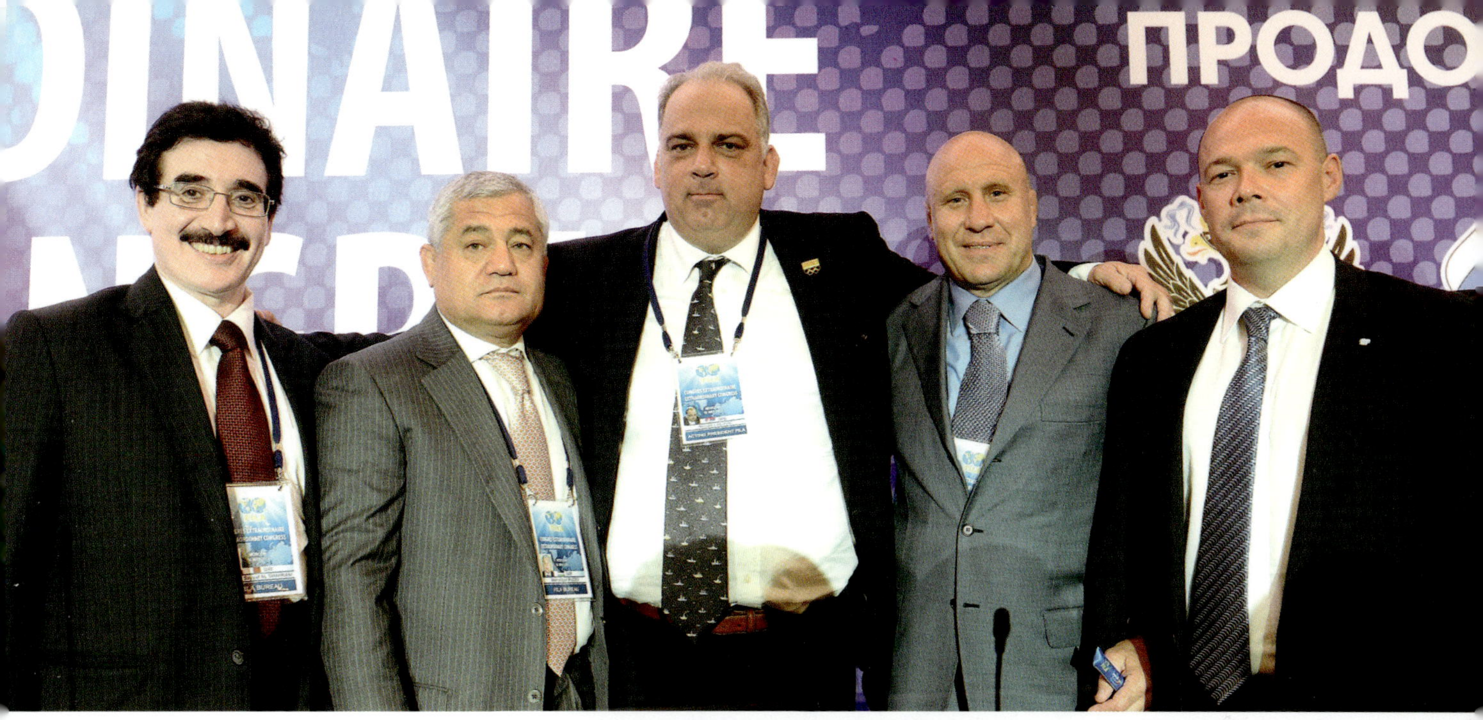

DAY 97:
BEAT THE STREETS LA & SEMNANI FAMILY FOUNDATION HOST **UNITED 4 WRESTLING**

May 19, Los Angeles, California

Wrestling under the recent rule changes adopted by FILA, athletes from Russia and the United States meet in Los Angeles for a dual meet at the Los Angeles Memorial Sports Arena.The event is a success with more than 7500 fans purchasing tickets. Though a late cancellation by the Iranian team threatens the event, organizers add matches and promote the inclusion of women and youth – a move that makes United 4 Wrestling one of most iconic events of the Save Olympic Wrestling movement.

Pictured: (Above) FILA Bureau members Zamel Sayyaf Al Shahrani (QAT) and Akhroldjan Ruziev (UKR) with FILA President Nenad Lalovic, Bureau Member Mikhail Mamiashvili and General Secretary of the Russian Wrestling Federation George Brusov. (Right) USA Wrestling team member Jordan Oliver.

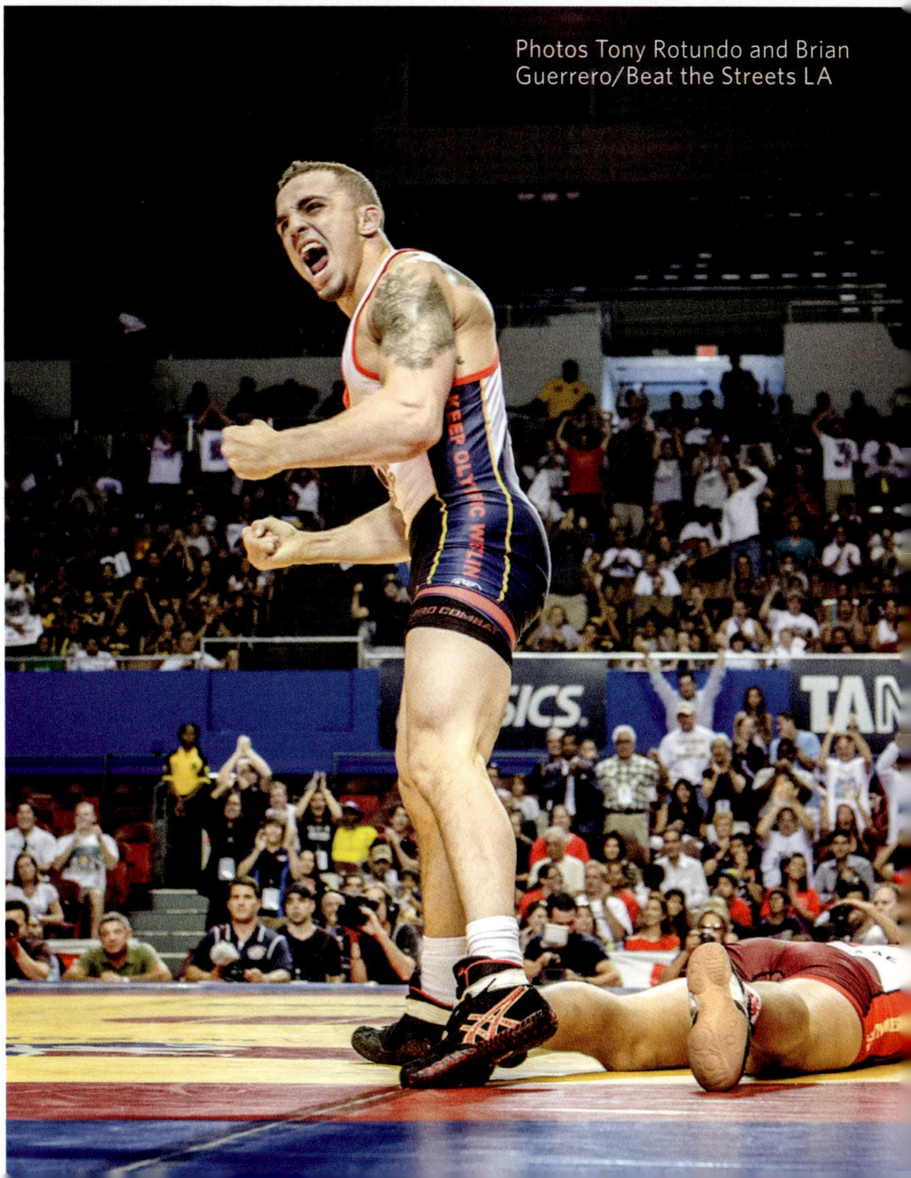

Photos Tony Rotundo and Brian Guerrero/Beat the Streets LA

SPONSORED BY THE
SEMNANI FAMILY FOUNDATION
INTERNATIONAL COMPETITION AT THE
LOS ANGELES MEMORIAL SPORTS ARENA

UNITED 4 WRESTLING

2020 Vision | Keep the Dream Alive

THE UNITED STATES OF AMERICA

ISLAMIC REPUBLIC OF IRAN

USA vs IRAN Dual Meet
May 19, 2013   Doors open at 1:00 pm
Los Angeles Memorial Sports Arena
3939 S. Figueroa Street, Los Angeles
Current International Freestyle Rule
Lineups to be released when available.

Tickets for the Event will be available at
Ticketmaster.com beginning May 1st

SEMNANI FAMILY FOUNDATION

USA wrestling

CALIFORNIA
USA
WRESTLING

BEAT
THE
STREETS
LOS ANGELES

Jordan Burroughs , a 2012 Olympic champion and two-time world champion, celebrates another victory in front of the American fans.

Former UFC Champion Randy Couture.

Artas Sanaa (RUS) looks to throw Sam Hazewinkel (USA).

Andy Barth, wrestling philanthropist and founder of the Titan Mercury WC, provided guidance and support throughout the Save Olympic Wrestling movement.

DAY 101:
WRESTLING REACTS WELL
TO CHALLENGE

May 23, Lausanne, Switzerland

In an interview with the Associated Press, IOC President Jacques Rogge says that wrestling has "reacted well" in its bid to preserve their Olympic status. The first vote, which prunes a list of eight candidate sports to three, is only five days away.

9 PEOPLE GATHERED
WRESTLING
013.5.15 PM 15:00
ING FEDERATION
East Japan College Wrestling Association

DAY 105:
SPORTACCORD MEETINGS AND PREPARATION

May 27, St. Petersburg, Russia

FILA announces the names of the five panelists that will participate in its presentation to the IOC Executive Board in St. Petersburg.

The panelists for the presentation are: FILA President Nenad Lalovic; Carol Huynh, a Canadian wrestler who won a gold medal at the 2008 Olympics and a bronze in the 2012 Games; Lise Legrand, Vice President of the French Wrestling Federation and a bronze medal winner in the 2004 Olympics; Daniel Igali, a Nigerian-Canadian who won a gold medal in the 2000 Games and is a member of Nigeria's provincial parliament; and Jim Scherr, the first Olympian to lead the U.S. Olympic Committee and a bronze medalist in the World Championships.

The same five members of the presentation team will also represent FILA at the September 8 IOC Session in Buenos Aires, Argentina.

FILA Bureau member Alexander Karelin (RUS).

DAY 105:
PHILIPPINES ENDORSES WRESTLING

May 27, Manila, Philippines

President of the Philippines Benigno Aquino III approves Republic Act 10588, which endorses wrestling as a high school sport.

DAY 106:
WRESTLING AMONG TOP THREE SPORTS

May 28, St. Petersburg, Russia

The IOC Executive Board selects wrestling among three sports for the short list of candidate sports for the final provisional sport spot in the 2020 and 2024 Olympic Games. The other sports named to the short list of sports are squash and baseball/softball.

The final three sports will present their sports to the full IOC General Assembly on September 8, with only one of those sports earning inclusion into the 2020 and 2024 Olympics.

While our place in the Olympic Games is still not guaranteed," says Lalovic. "This decision recognizes the great lengths to which we are going to reform our sport and address the IOC's concerns."

Pictured: (Left) Nenad Lalovic, Jim Scherr, Carol Huynh.

SA MAJESTE LE ROI MOHAMMED VI
MONDE DE LUTTE DE PLAGE
GRE

Fitco
Fitco
attica bank

DAY 109:
BATTLE AT THE FALLS

May 31, Niagara Falls, Ontario, Canada

Wrestling Canada hosts the "Battle At The Falls," a women's freestyle wrestling event in Niagara Falls, Canada. Teams from the USA and Ukraine join the Canadians to compete in dual meets in front of one of the world's most iconic locations. The Canadian team is led by World champion Jessica MacDonald at 51 kg and two-time World bronze medalist Justine Bouchard at 63 kg.

The event reaffirms the wrestling community's commitment to expanding the opportunities for women in the future of international wrestling.

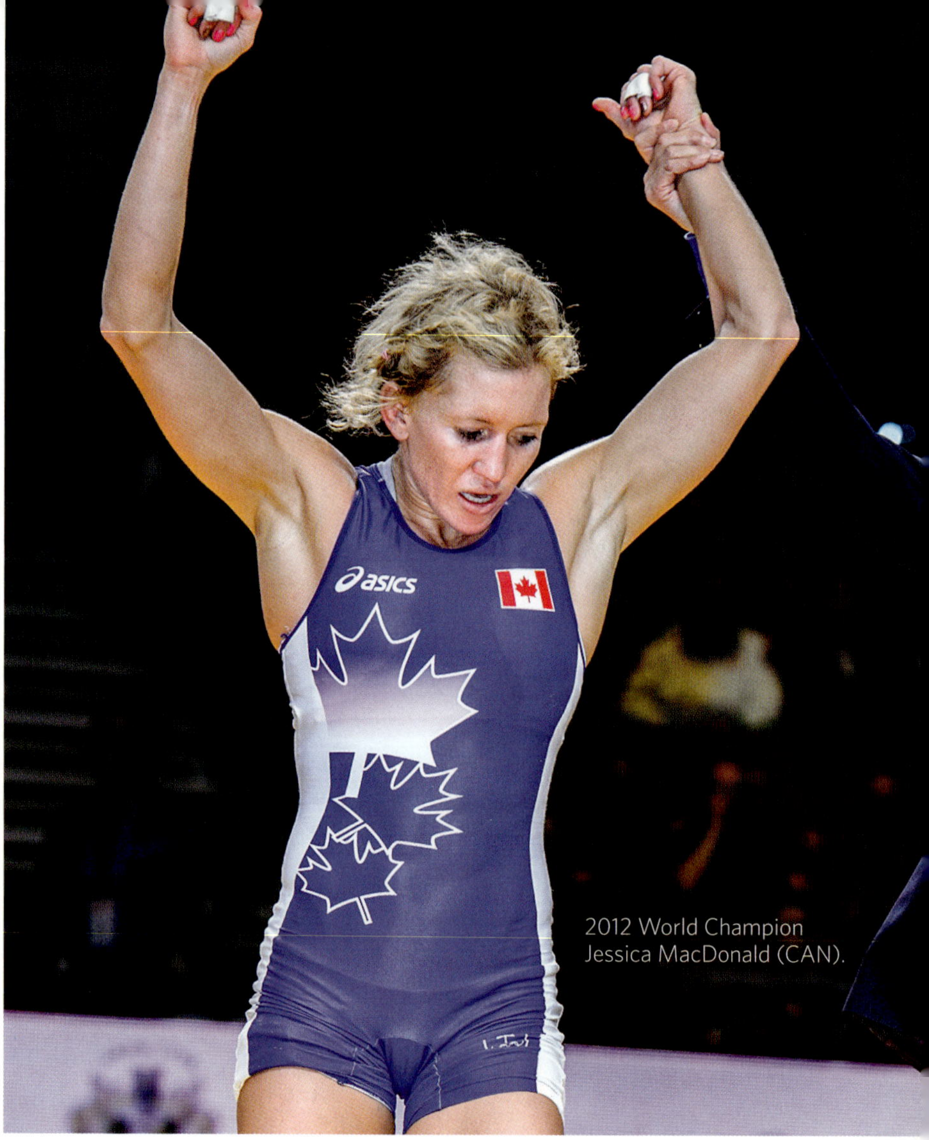

2012 World Champion Jessica MacDonald (CAN).

2013 INTERNATIONAL BATTLE AT THE FALLS WOMEN'S WRESTLING DUALS

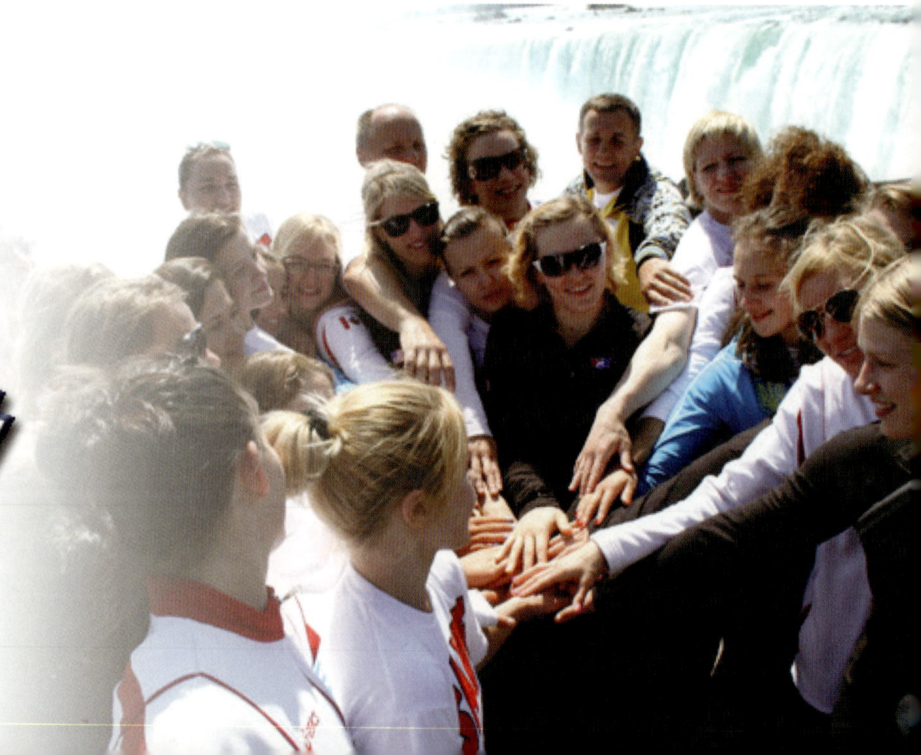

DAY 122:
ASIAN JUNIOR CHAMPIONSHIPS
June 13, Phuket, Thailand
One of the toughest continental championships, the Asian Junior Championships welcomes wrestlers from across Asia, including teams from Myanmar, Thailand and Vietnam.

DAY 126:
CPOW SUMMIT

June 17, Chicago, Illinois

Bill and Jim Scherr call on leaders within the Save Olympic Wrestling movement to a full day of meetings in Chicago. Olympic champions Dan Gable and FILA Vice President member Stan Dziedzic join with USA Wrestling executive director Rich Bender in a spirited discussion on the new rules, FILA governance and what can be done to promote the sport over the final months of the campaign.

Pictured: (Right) FILA Bureau Member Stan Dziedzic (USA). (Below) 2012 Olympic Champion shoots a double leg against Kyle Dake in the 74 kg finals of the WTT.

DAY 128:
CPOW INVESTS IN **WORLD TEAM TRIALS**

June 19, Stillwater, Oklahoma

Looking for an opportunity to garner support in the wrestling community, CPOW puts money into the United States' World Team Trials. Buoyed by the closely contested men's freestyle bracket at 74kg, the event proves to be a success, generating increased support and awareness for the campaign and the dreams of America's Olympic wrestlers.

Photos Tony Rotundo

Ryan Mango (Red) looks for a throw against Jesse Thielke (Blue).

Alyssa Lampe (Red) defends the attack of Victoria Anthony (Blue).

DAY 151:
PAN AM **JUNIOR** **CHAMPIONSHIPS**

July 12, Santiago, Chile

Proving that wrestling is everywhere, the Pan American Junior Championships provide wrestlers from South America the opportunity to show their wrestling skill against teams from North and Central America. Many of the wrestlers in attendance are on teams subsidized by FILA who invests hundreds of thousands of dollars every year in the expanding wrestling's reach in countries who otherwise can't afford wrestling programs. FILA also opens discussions into expanding Olympic solidarity within South America.

Kevin Mejia, a Greco-Roman wrestler from Honduras, stares down his opponent in early round action. Meijia is a Pan-Am Junior gold medalist and 2012 Cadet world bronze medalist.

Adam Ludwin (USA) in the freestyle finals at 55 kg. looking for a go-behind against Andy Davila (VEN).

ΣΥΛΛΟΓΟΣ ΟΛΥΜΠΙΟΝΙΚΩΝ
ΗΡΑΚΛΗΣ
ΠΕΡΙΣΤΕΡΙΟΥ

DAY 158:
WRESTLING IN
ANCIENT OLYMPIA

July 19, Olympia, Athens, Greece

Wrestlers from around the world gather at the birthplace of the Olympic movement to participate in a Senior International Tournament. The gathering of wrestlers represents the themes of the Save Olympic Wrestling campaign: wrestling is universal, wrestling is for everyone and wrestling is one of the original sports.

Male and female wrestlers from Albania, Brazil, Germany, Great Britain, Greece, Iran, Russia and the United States, all compete in the event. Several youth wrestlers also compete on the grounds of the palaestra, making history as the first to compete in the area since the end of the Ancient Olympic Games era in 393 B.C. Two female youth athletes that took part in the exhibition were the first-ever female athletes to wrestle in Ancient Olympia.

Helen Maroulis (USA), one of the first women to wrestle on the grounds of Ancient Olympia.

TITAN
ΑΝΤΩΝΗΣ ΠΑΝΤΑΦΥΛΛΟΠΟΥΛΟΣ
TITAN
ΤΟΥ

WR
SOS
SAVE OLYMPIC WRESTLING
CAIXA

Wrestlers in the finals of the tournament wrestled in front of large crowds on the grounds of Ancient Olympia.

Save Olympic
WRESTLING

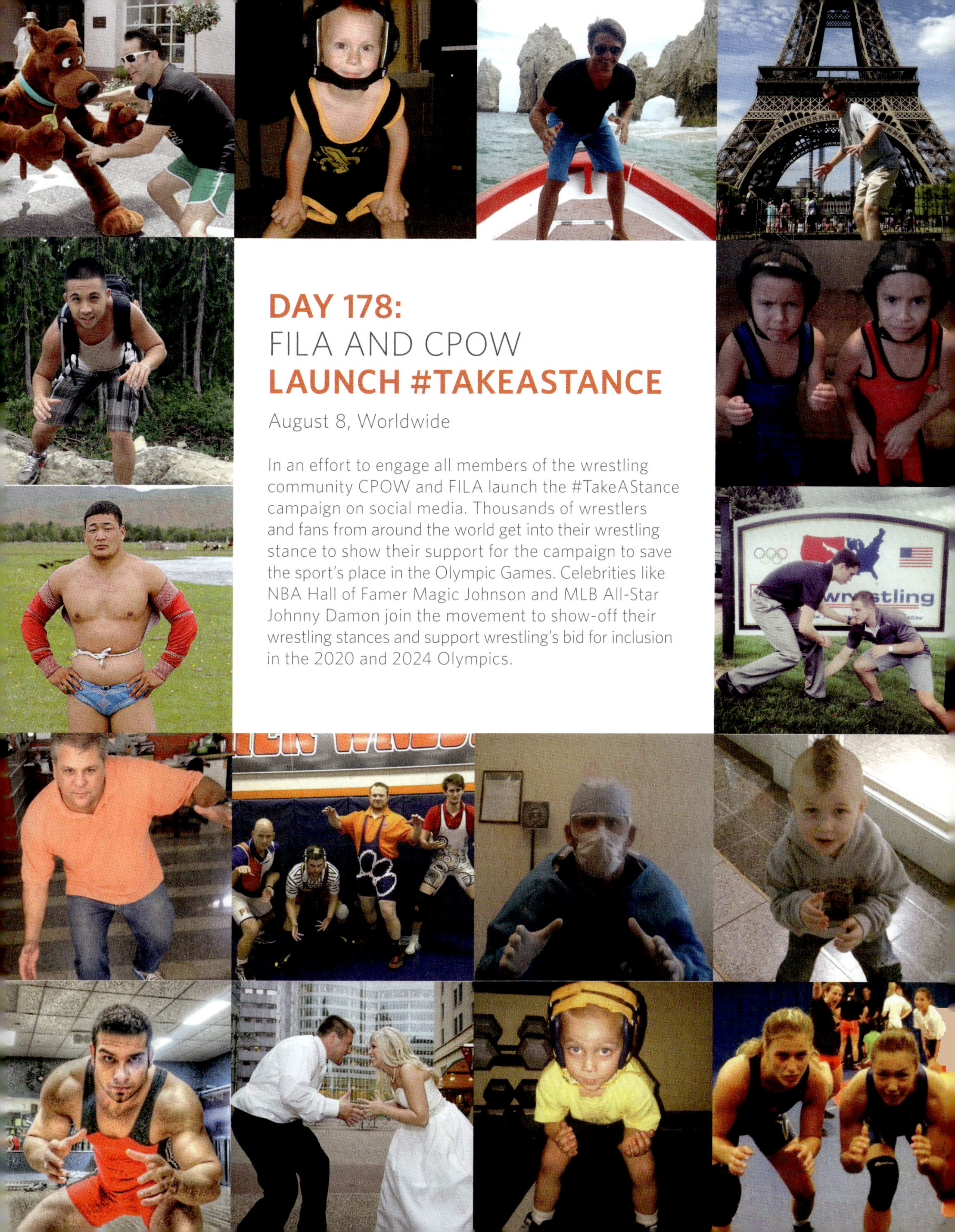

DAY 178:
FILA AND CPOW
LAUNCH #TAKEASTANCE

August 8, Worldwide

In an effort to engage all members of the wrestling community CPOW and FILA launch the #TakeAStance campaign on social media. Thousands of wrestlers and fans from around the world get into their wrestling stance to show their support for the campaign to save the sport's place in the Olympic Games. Celebrities like NBA Hall of Famer Magic Johnson and MLB All-Star Johnny Damon join the movement to show-off their wrestling stances and support wrestling's bid for inclusion in the 2020 and 2024 Olympics.

#TakeAStance

DAY 179:
FILA APPROVES
6-6-6 FOR RIO

August 9, Corsier-Sur-Vevey, Switzerland

In one of the most powerful moments of the Save Olympic Wrestling movement, FILA President Nenad Lalovic announces that international wrestling will move to a new 6-6-6 format for the 2016 Olympic Games in Rio de Janeiro. The announcement means that Greco-Roman, men's freestyle and women's freestyle will each have an equal number of Olympic weight classes.

Pictured: 2013 World bronze medalist
O. Nasanburmaa (MGL).

Photos: Tony Rotundo

2012 Olympic Champion
Natalia Vorobieva (RUS).

Three-time
Olympic Champion
Saori Yoshida (JPN).

2012 World Champion
Elena Pirozhkova (USA).

DAY 183:
JUNIOR WORLD
CHAMPIONSHIPS

August 13, Sofia, Bulgaria

The Bulgarian Wrestling Federation hosts the 2013 Junior World Championships in Sofia. The event draws thousands of fans and crowns several new Junior World Champions in men's freestyle, Greco-Roman and women's freestyle.

Pictured: (Right) Linda Morais (CAN) battles Katarzyna Madrowska (POL) in early round action. (Below) FILA President Nenad Lalovic, Bulgarian President Rusan Plevniev and 1996 Olympic champion Valentin Jordanov.

DAY 190:
CADET WORLD
WRESTLING
CHAMPIONSHIPS

August 20, Zrenjanin, Serbia

The Serbian Wrestling Federation welcomes wrestlers from around the world for a week of competition among the best Cadet-level wrestlers on the planet. Lalovic, who calls Serbia home, welcomes guests and does days worth of publicity to keep the attention on FILA's mission to secure a spot in the Olympics.

Pictured: (Above) 2013 Cadet World Champion Aaron Pico (USA), 63 kg. (Left) FILA Cadet silver medalist, Regina Doi (USA), 40 kg.

DAY 203: RALLY FOR WRESTLING

September 2, Atlanta, Georgia

CPOW and leaders from USA Wrestling come together for a send-off for wrestlers competing at the 2013 World Championships in Budapest. The event includes a wrestling clinic and autograph session with members of the United States national team.

Pictured: (Right) 1972 Olympic gold medalist Dan Gable. (Below) Rally 4 Wrestling's Wayne Boyd (L) and John Bardis (R) sit with 1996 Olympic gold medalist Tom Brands.

Photo: Milena (Ujkic) Wick

DAY 206:
WRESTLING LEADERS GATHER IN ARGENTINA

September 5, Buenos Aires, Argentina

The USA wrestling community gathers in Buenos Aires, Argentina to assist in the final days of the campaign to Save Olympic Wrestling. Actor Billy Baldwin joins Rich Bender, James Ravannack, Bill Scherr and members of FILA's presentation team for the final few days of preparation. Wrestling leaders from Russia, Japan, and countries throughout Europe, Asia and South America also show up to offer their support.

Pictured: (Below) Carol Huynh (CAN), Billy Baldwin, Lise LeGrand (FRA), Nenad Lalovic, Daniel Igali (CAN).

DAY 209:
WRESTLING VOTED INTO 2020 & 2024 GAMES

September 8, Buenos Aires, Argentina

Wrestling completes its comeback story by earning a resounding first-round vote by the IOC in its Session on September 8. FILA President Nenad Lalovic expresses the organization's satisfaction following the IOC's vote to keep wrestling in the Olympic Games.

"I want to offer my sincere gratitude to each member of the International Olympic Committee that voted to save Olympic wrestling today," says Lalovic. "With this vote, you have shown that the steps we have taken to improve our sport have made a difference. I assure each of you that our modernization will not stop now. We will continue to strive to be the best partner to the Olympic Movement that we can be."

"To the millions of wrestlers, supporters and fans around the world that came together to save Olympic wrestling, I offer a very big thank you," says Lalovic. "Every one of you fought very hard for this victory. Now we must remain united to make certain we live up to the expectations that have been placed on all of us by virtue of this vote."

Pictured: (Above) FILA President Nenad Lalovic and Alexander Karelin (RUS) moments after the IOC vote. (Right) Nenad Lalovic with FILA Bureau Member Rodica Yaksi (TUR).

Photos: Alexander Orechnov and Tony Rotundo

Jim Scherr (USA), Daniel Igali (CAN), Lise LeGrand (FRA), Carol Huynh (CAN) and FILA President Nenad Lalovic.

Greco-Roman wrestler Ryu Han-Su (KOR) celebrates
his 2013 World Championship at 66 kg.

Elmurat Tasmuradov (UZB) looks to block the lift of Almat Kebispayev (KAZ) in the bronze medal Greco-Roman match at 66 kg.

asics
EURO-PROFIL
www.europrofil.hu

Greco-Roman wrestler Viktor Lorincz (HUN) celebrates his bronze medal victory at 84 kg in front of his home crowd in Budapest.

Kanybek Kholchubekov (KGZ) lifts Jario Medina Garcia (VEN) at the 2013 World Championships.

Greco-Roman wrestler Frank Staebler (GER) celebrates his bronze medal at the 2013 World Championships.

The László Papp Sports Arena in Budapest, host of the 2013 Wrestling World Championships.

Sandeep Tulsi Yadan (66 kg) jumps into his coach's arms after becoming India's first-ever world medalist in Greco-Roman wrestling.

Yun Won-Chol (PRK) became North Korea's first-ever world champion in Greco-Roman wrestling, winning the 55 kg weight class in Budapest, Hungary.

Afterword

"We shall not cease from exploration, and the end of all our exploring will be to arrive where we started and know the place for the first time."

—T. S. Eliot

It only took one ballot for wrestling to be voted back into the Olympics. One ballot, $10 million, and the efforts of 20 million wrestlers.

In the weeks and months following the IOC vote in Buenos Aires, Argentina, FILA president Nenad Lalovic pushed for more adjustments to the sport of wrestling. After a successful World Championships in Budapest, Hungary, the Serbian leader asked FILA membership to approve rule changes and add women and athletes to the FILA Bureau. Not every rule change was well received, but FILA started to show the IOC that they were going to make changes and bolster their commitment to the IOC, rather than limit interaction.

Today, the future of the wrestling is more certain than it was on February 12, 2013, but the battle for full Olympic partnership marches on. Although wrestling is back in the 2020 and 2024 Games, the IOC vote in Buenos Aires made no guarantees for wrestling's presence at the 2028 Olympics. To ensure the sport's overall survival, wrestling will need to lobby and show the membership of the IOC that wrestling wants to be a full and active member. Wrestling will need to increase television viewership, improve the fan experience, and expand its marketing campaign.

Work remains, but with new leadership and marketable ideas being generated by leaders around the world, wrestling is poised for a revival of its centuries old Olympic popularity.

Acknowledgements

Cover Design: Cliff Fretwell
Cover Photos: Tony Rotundo

Photo Credits

Day 1: Tony Rotundo
Day 3: (T) Placeit.net; (B) T. R. Foley
Day 6: T.R. Foley
Day 8: Tony Rotundo
Day 9: FILA
Day 16: Amir Pourman
Day 18: Sven Teschke
Day 24: FILA
Day 25: Tony Rotundo
Day 26: T.R. Foley
Day 30: Kremlin.ru
Day 36: Tony Rotundo
Day 38: Tony Rotundo
Day 38: FILA
Day 39: Press Conference, Tony Rotundo;
Varner/Burroughs, Larry Slater
Day 42: Martin Gabor/FILA
Day 45: Alexander Orechnov
Day 46: USA Wrestling
Day 47: T.R. Foley
Day 50: (T) Tony Rotundo,
(B) USA Wrestling
Day 51: T.R. Foley
Day 52: Larry Slater
Day 53: Marie-Lan Nguyen
Day 54: Wrestrus.Ru (L) T.R. Foley
Day 59: Tony Rotundo
Day 60: Japan Wrestling Federation
Day 65: Alexander Orechnov
Day 66: T.R. Foley
Day 69: Dan Gable, Tony Rotundo; Traditional
Wrestlers, T.R. Foley

Day 79: USA Wrestling
Day 80: Traditional Wrestlers, T.R. Foley;
Olympic Wrestlers, Alexander Orechnov
Day 87: Dakota Fine; Henry Cejudo,
Tony Rotundo
Day 89: C. Ganbat
Day 92: Noel Thompson
Day 93: John Sachs
Day 96: Alexander Orechnov
Day 97: Andy Barth, Brian Guerrero, Beat the
Streets LA; all other photos, Tony Rotundo
Day 101: Japan Wrestling Federation
Day 105, Manilla: Ashkan Ghaedramat
Day 105, St. Petersburg: Alexander Orechnov
Day 106: Squash, Amey Khanolkar;
Baseball, Victor Grigas
Day 109, El-Jadida: Ujjwal Kumar
Day 109, Niagara Falls: Jessica MacDonald,
Tony Rotundo; Group Shot, USA Wrestling
Day 122: T.R. Foley
Day 126: Tony Rotundo
Day 128: Tony Rotundo
Day 151: T.R. Foley
Day 158: Angelos Zymaras/FILA
Day 164: C. Ganbat
Day 179: Tony Rotundo
Day 183: Action photo, FILA;
Group photo, T.R. Foley
Day 190: T.R. Foley
Day 203: Milena (Ujkic) Wick
Day 206: Top: Noel Thompson,
Bottom, T.R. Foley
Day 209: Left: Tony Rotundo;
Right, Alexander Orechnov
Afterword: Tony Rotundo